THE SCHOOL AND
THE WORLD COMMUNITY SERIES

PAMPHLET NO. I

THE
TEACHING OF GEOGRAPHY
IN RELATION TO THE
WORLD COMMUNITY

CAMBRIDGE

Published for the
Advisory Education Committee for Wales
(League of Nations Union)

AT THE UNIVERSITY PRESS

1933

CAMBRIDGE
UNIVERSITY PRESS

University Printing House, Cambridge CB2 8BS, United Kingdom

Cambridge University Press is part of the University of Cambridge.

It furthers the University's mission by disseminating knowledge in the pursuit of education, learning and research at the highest international levels of excellence.

www.cambridge.org
Information on this title: www.cambridge.org/9781316633243

First published 1933
First paperback edition 2016

A catalogue record for this publication is available from the British Library

ISBN 978-1-316-63324-3 Paperback

CONTENTS

GENERAL NOTE

THE pamphlets in "The School and the World Community Series" are not intended to unloose yet another flood of advice and information upon teachers already overwhelmed by books "of the making of which there is no end". The series aims merely at suggesting a point of view. To many teachers this point of view may be new—to others it may be obvious.

But, from a long and varied experience of schools and teaching, the Editor is convinced that an occasional examination of motive is necessary in order to prevent the warm living flesh of wisdom being replaced by the dry lifeless bones of formal instruction.

The title "The School and World Community Series" almost explains itself. The purpose of the series is to suggest to teachers of every subject in the school curriculum how to think about that subject, firstly in its relation to the constructive contributions of different peoples to the world's culture in general, and secondly in association with the fact that the world is a community of peoples whose greatest need to-day is sympathetic understanding and co-operation.

Thus the booklets in this series attempt to set teachers thinking about their work in relation, not merely to their own country, but to the world community as well. The booklets do not provide working material: they are signposts not roads. They seek only to discuss in outline the way to give a world setting to certain of the workaday subjects of the school, and to refer to sources of information. Teachers, especially, have to realise that in the modern world we are members one of another and that we cannot afford in the schools to ignore this truth. The interdependence of the nations is a commonplace fact which is taken so much for granted that it is seldom realised and yet is so vital to the well-being of everyone that we cannot give it too much emphasis in any liberal system of education.

October 1933   FREDERIC EVANS

PREFATORY NOTE

BY H. J. FLEURE

EDUCATION IS OUR PREPARATION FOR LIFE, AND we are called upon to try to build up a vision of our world which shall have a good measure of reality and an appreciation of the forces that have made and are ever remaking us as we are and are becoming. This means that education must adapt itself from age to age, and that great changes in the world inevitably involve changing developments of education that may sometimes be revolutionary in magnitude. It is obvious that we are now in one of those times of revolution and that its bearing on education needs to be considered seriously. Without gleaning too widely, one may cite some western European examples of past modes of education and the crises involved as they met great world changes.

In what are called the Middle Ages western Europe was recovering from a phase of poverty and attendant disorder that came after the fall of the Roman Empire and the cutting of the old trade routes of the Mediterranean through the advance of Islam. Men in Europe were needing to learn to improve their craftsmanship in agriculture, building, furnishing, cooking, civic and regional life; and they were covering over a multitude of local traditions, that had furnished motives for action, with the teaching of the Christian Church. This furnished at any rate a bigger generalisation than any of the local mythologies and it was full of motive power for social life and organisation at any rate in the phase of the popular enthusiasm of the twelfth and thirteenth centuries. That education in this period emphasised craftsmanship on the one hand and religion on the other is thus most natural. Further, one can trace the increasing effect of logical thought working upon the foundation of poetic enthusiasm as well as the growth of vested interests making obstacles to free adventure in thought and action. It is not necessary to enquire whether mediaevalism would have died of itself: a crisis came and it passed away. Gutenberg, through the art of printing, brought ideas to a mass of people previously untouched, and led them first to enquire into the sources of the Christian tradition and those of the Roman order, the two largest elements of their spiritual heritage. Classical Greek culture thus came to have an immense influence among the learned, but, through the translation of the Bible, the vernaculars of the people acquired new value and became vehicles of education that was to make peoples speaking one language conscious of that which drew them together and separated them from the rest of mankind. Classical education, built up on leisure was for the privileged few, craftsmanship and religion, but now assisted with the mother tongue in many parts of Europe, for the many. The mother tongue became the binding force of nationality, the root of patriotism to blossom forth as nationalism in its extreme development in the treaties framed after November 1918 when world changes were already calling aloud for other ideas. Linguistic nationalism with a more or less religious background, however it was tempered by a classical education common to the leisured few in the various nations, had long become inadequate ere the treaties of 1918–19 crowned it amid hymns of hate.

Already as Gutenberg's work was beginning, another revolution of slower maturation was preparing itself. Copernicus showed that the blue sky was not a curtain separating us from the Judgment Throne but, rather, an effect of the unmeasured depths of space; and Henry the Navigator and Columbus superseded the mediaeval map with its little world centred around Jerusalem. There was a new vision of the universe and of a world to be filled in and new and distant sources of wealth to be brought into circulation.

The old patriotism might be of use so long as a people lived mainly to itself, deriving its sustenance from its own fields and its equipment from its own craftsmen working on home materials. Its limitations became painfully evident when contacts with Amerindians and Africans were multiplied and oppression and slavery stained once more the name of

Christianity. The strength of the patriotic sentiment hindered the growth of any regulation of exchanges between peoples; and even now it is rarely realised that the acquisition of great fortunes through international trade is a serious difficulty, and one of the larger factors of the economic crisis which has been brewing for the last 40 years and is developing so seriously in 1933.

Out of the investigations which grew after Copernicus and Columbus had superannuated the mediaeval vision, came, in the end of the eighteenth century, the revolution due to the application of power on a scale hitherto unknown, perhaps the greatest economic change since the age of great inventions when agriculture was organising itself and the stone age was about to pass into that of copper and bronze. Printing and paper were cheapened and the vernacular literatures acquired new power, adding hot fuel to the nationalist fires fanned by newspaper polemics. Translations became widespread, and others besides the privileged few of the old grand tours came to know something of other peoples and too often to exploit that knowledge for ambitious ends. Our daily life came to depend on goods from the ends of the earth, and exchanges were so conducted as to lead some peoples into a debtor and others into a creditor position, with over-development of these features on both sides and consequent attempts at protection of the individuality of a group endangered by economic or other dependence.

In this complex situation, with the peoples of the world jostling one another day by day and irritating one another by their diversities of convention, and with financial ambitions almost beyond control, it is obvious that we must try to know all we can of one another, of our need of one another, of our relations with our various homelands, and of the supplements we need from other lands and peoples, in ideas as well as objects, if we are to maintain and develop the good life.

It is but too clear that *laissez-faire* failed as a theory and has joined the museum of social and economic fossils, but there is little skill and less experience in planning for social and economic welfare. The Russian exponents of the new art admit that they are struggling with the catastrophic failure of the agricultural part of their plans. Germany, England and America are equally struggling with catastrophic failures of schemes of employment and of circulation of wealth.

A study of the peoples of the world is called for ever more insistently in school and university and also in the world's chancelleries. We shall need much thought and patience and the casting away of many tawdry ambitions ere the peoples of the world, each living in appropriate numbers to a considerable extent on the resources of its own home, can exchange with other peoples without fear of economic or political subjection in such a way as to enrich its life.

Study will doubtless reveal that there is a strong case for specialisation of many peoples, and, while what we call geography can help here, it has to be left to other branches of study to work out how specialisation may in future be regulated to avoid the disproportionate accumulation of credits at one end and debits at the other.

I

RACIAL PREJUDICES AMONGST SCHOOL CHILDREN

BY GEORGE H. GREEN

THE DEVELOPMENT OF AERIAL TRANSIT AND OF wireless means of communication are but the latest and most dramatic phases of a process which has been going on for centuries, tending towards the unification of the world. Already the world has shrunk to the dimensions of a small country. Who, taking into account the accelerated progress of mechanical invention, can say how little a space of time will be necessary for its conversion to a village?

With this development has necessarily gone an increasing dependence of any one part of the world on all the others. We, in Britain, depend upon all the countries of the earth for our food, our clothing, our materials for the provision of shelter, our fuel—our necessities and our luxuries. To the same extent, even if not in precisely the same way, the nations of the earth depend upon Britain and the British Empire for the means of life. Even if "world citizenship" is an ideal rather than a fact, it is nevertheless true that, wittingly or unwittingly, the nations of the world are co-operating with each other in every phase of the complex life of to-day. And it is very clear that the future of the world is bound up, for good or ill, with the development and conscious direction of international co-operation.

Recognition of this fact does not commit us to the approval of the means which have been devised up to the present for the organisation of international co-operation, or to whole-hearted support of existing institutions planned to direct international affairs. It does, however, make us realise that hatred, suspicion and fear of peoples of other races and nations place obstacles in the way of co-operation. Respect, candour and confidence are essential to co-operation, whether of individuals or of nations.

Thus it appears to be of great importance to enquire what are the attitudes of young children—children of school age—towards the people of races and nationalities other than their own. The obvious reply to this is that children of school age KNOW little or nothing of alien races and nations, and will therefore not feel towards them. This answer is, however, an expression of opinion, and no more. The question must be submitted to the test of investigation before we can be certain about the matter.

Children's attitudes towards alien peoples have been investigated here and there by several enquirers. Varying techniques, of differing degrees of reliability, have been employed. Some of the experiments have been carried out with fairly large numbers of children, others with a few only. What can be said with confidence at the present moment is that large numbers of children of school age, in Britain and the United States of America, believe good and ill of peoples on the sole ground of membership of a racial or national group; and express opinions showing that they regard whole races and nations with suspicion, hatred or fear.

One investigation, which will have to be repeated in other parts of the world before wide generalisations can be based upon it, suggests that the attitudes of secondary school pupils of seventeen and eighteen years of age are not markedly different from those of school children of eight: the prejudices are exactly the same, but are defended with more ingenuity. It was found, in the course of the investigation referred to, that when preferences or prejudices were challenged, children made statements which they considered to justify their attitudes—statements which were traceable to the home, to books, to direct contacts with foreign people, to the school, to newspapers, to religious institutions and to the cinema.[1]

It is clear that we are here dealing with a matter which

[1] For a full report of this investigation, see *The Welsh Outlook* for March, April, May and June, 1930. (The Welsh Outlook Press: Newtown, Mid-Wales. Price 2s. for the four issues.)

deserves very full psychological investigation. The capacity to love, to fear, to suspect, to feel jealousy, to hate, would be regarded by many psychologists as parts of the child's innate endowment. In all cases, probably, the child first displays these attitudes during infancy towards people in the home circle and towards strangers he meets. Often he shows fear and suspicion of people, merely because they behave "strangely", i.e. differently from the people he loves and trusts. The question of the ways in which these tendencies are directed towards peoples of whom the child knows little or nothing is, in all probability, partly psychological and partly social: it is, in any case, one which urgently requires answering. Until we know the answer, we cannot hope to introduce any efficient means of control.[1]

Meanwhile, it is worth remarking that in the statements made by children to justify their preferences for certain alien peoples above others, they referred frequently to the "kindness" of the people who grew bananas and other fruits, or who made toys for them. This appreciation of indebtedness is all to the good, though it may be questioned whether children should be encouraged to believe naïvely that the end and purpose of the existence of the people who inhabit the tropics is to provide the British table with luxuries. Nevertheless, the child who has learned of his dependence upon the negro cultivator of fruits and cotton and sugar and upon the continental toymaker is at the beginning of the realisation of the unity of mankind.

It is an educational commonplace that one cannot destroy an opinion by contradicting it. Contradiction by the teacher is likely to do little more than impress on the child that there are two kinds of truth—one right and proper for the classroom; the other for the outside world. The wrong opinion lives on in undiminished strength.

[1] The New Education Fellowship has appointed a world commission to deal with the whole question of Education for International Understanding, and to present at least an interim report to the World Conference of New Education in 1935. The commission will, as part of its work, initiate enquiries into this problem. Information regarding the commission and its work may be obtained from The Commissions Secretary, New Education Fellowship, 29 Tavistock Square, London, W.C. 1.

Meanwhile, much can be done in various ways in the school to show that international co-operation is a fact, without adding another subject to the curriculum or making special provision in the time-table. The study of the letters of the alphabet, for example, shows that we owe them eventually to the work of peoples of different races, co-operating with each other, unwittingly and over long periods of time. The same thing is true of the symbols we use in arithmetic and of arithmetical processes. The story of Algebra, if we accept its Arabic origin, is one of co-operation in which every nation of importance has taken a share.

The story of Science is a similar one. Indeed, there is no subject of the school curriculum which cannot be correctly interpreted as the outcome of international co-operation. In every instance we can point to this co-operation, at first unwitting and undirected, and only recently deliberate and organised. We can point, too, to the good results that follow from conscious direction.

We may contrast the slow progress of studies in periods of history when contacts between the peoples of the world were few and difficult, when development was at a standstill till new contacts were made. It is easy to show, for example, that in the last century more progress was made in the field of science than in all the centuries which preceded it; and this because the scientists of the world, during this period, increasingly organised themselves in ways which enabled them to know of the work of one another. For this reason we were able, in a comparatively short space of time, to solve the problems of wireless communication, of aerial transport, of sound recording and reproduction, and a host of others—not less important, though of less interest to school children.

The teacher of geography, too, may specially direct his teaching towards making his pupils conscious of the part played in the world of to-day by international co-operation, since he has to speak of the varied products of the earth and of the means of communication between the different parts of the world. And, as he speaks of the physical aspects of the natural regions, so he will be compelled to point out that these play their part in imposing upon the men who inhabit them a "way of life"— a "culture", in the anthropological sense of the word. This "culture", though an integral whole, is many-sided, presenting many aspects which, though they cannot exist in isolation, can nevertheless be studied separately. And thus, through intelligent treatment of the subject, the pupil comes to know that customs which appear strange— even revolting—to us have not originated in the love of queer and revolting things, but are capable of being understood. We do not approve of them because we understand them; but we realise that administrators of backward peoples are more likely to meet with success when they understand the object of customs which have to be changed—when they are able to discover, as has frequently been the case, new directions for the energies formerly expended in other ways. A precise parallel may be discovered in the way in which the energies of boys have been directed, in the case of Boy Scouts, through the understanding of the founder of the movement, away from channels of aimless "mischief" and turned towards purposeful activity.

Much may be done, then, without interference with the work of the school and without excessive demand upon those working within it, to make pupils realise the essential unity of mankind, to make them aware of the world as a single unit, and to lead them to regard the peoples of the world with understanding. Understanding does much to remove suspicion and fear and hatred, and thus contributes to the breaking down of the barriers which stand in the way of fruitful international co-operation. Further, the existing results of international co-operation can be so presented that a desire to co-operate is fostered, and this in itself becomes an incentive to knowledge of the peoples of the world.

A remark on the ways in which the peoples of the world are commonly presented to children seems called for. Parents, teachers and writers of text-books alike might be asked to consider the question—If you wished to present the children of England, Wales, Scotland or Ireland fairly to the children of Turkey, what material would you use? Would you select all that was odd and queer and strange, and repress all that seemed ordinary and usual? Would you illustrate the life of the English child of to-day by reference to the Maypole and to country dances? Would you confine yourself to remarks applying to one social class only, or to a single occupation? Would your illustrations be limited to those showing children in costumes of a bygone age, or men and women wearing costumes which are rarely worn, on special occasions?

When all these questions have been answered, it might be well to enquire why people often persist in attempting to give children an idea of the Dutch people through the medium of an odd child in the odd costume of a Volendam fisherman, or why the German is still almost exclusively presented either as a Prussian guardsman or an obese peasant with a porcelain tobacco-pipe. True, satisfactory material dealing with the real lives of the people of other races and nations is urgently wanted. When it is urgently demanded, it will probably be forthcoming. But, until it is ready for the child, and until a desire to use it is fostered and stimulated, we can hardly wonder that his attitudes towards foreign peoples are wrong and stupid; and that he remains susceptible to any propaganda against alien peoples which may from time to time be organised by unscrupulous individuals, desirous of exploiting his credulity for their own ends.

II

GEOGRAPHY AND WORLD CITIZENSHIP[1]

BY CELIA EVANS

THE GREAT WAR REDIRECTED THE CONSCIENCE and the consciousness of the world towards the problem of conciliation and co-operation. In this work it is perhaps the historians who have been most to the fore. The conception of history as a school subject has, within the last ten years or so, been slowly developing from a purely national to a world conception. This great change is manifest in books,

[1] Reprinted from *The New Era*.

in official publications, in syllabuses, and in teaching. What then of geography?

Geography, as its name implies, is supremely a world subject. It is surely *the* subject to develop in its devotees an understanding of the world. But it has not always done so. The familiar "capes and bays" phase of geography teaching made of the subject a jig-saw puzzle wherein knowledge of situations on a mere outline map was the limited end in view. There was no clear association of the printed form and symbol with the country behind them and with the *people* inhabiting the land concerned. It was factual, unrelated knowledge and distasteful at that. Then geography often came to mean, mainly, the learning of facts about the British Empire. The idea of "possessions" was emphasised. Misleading Mercator projections were used in the world maps to exaggerate these "possessions" which were coloured gaudily in red. Often, too, this phase of geography teaching laid more stress upon frontiers than upon relief and regions. The "expansion" theory of progress in a State, so definitely a creed of the nineteenth century, left its mark on ideas in the teaching of geography. The industrial growth of Britain in the same period emphasised the necessity of "markets" which were visualised mainly as colonial markets or markets in our "possessions".

The Great War brought this phase to a close. The tendencies of the colonies towards virtual self-government had their fullest expression in the colonies' co-operation in the War as separate entities and in the peace as separate members of the League of Nations. The fallacy of "owning" colonies was ended; co-operation rather than competition became the conscious need, if not the conscious aim, of the world. Tariff barriers which tend to separate the nations economically, still, however, exist to interfere with world co-operation as a wholly natural thing. Political interference with trade and commerce is still a disquieting feature in the post-War world, and this tends usually to run counter to the influences operating towards unity. M. Briand's "United States of Europe" met with philosophical approval but practical opposition. We have yet far to go. In creating a world point of view in these matters, geography is clearly the school subject wherein this can best be done.

In the past, also, geography has been too much concerned in the schools with bringing out the *differences* between peoples rather than the vastly greater number of *likenesses* which exist between them. The schools have been more apt to point out that a negro is black than that he is a man. This emphasis on differences is undoubtedly the main factor in the general failure of geography teaching to produce a world mind. Even the *differences* of culture, of habit, of language, of outlook and so on among peoples can be referred to as giving to the world that necessary variety which means vitality. Each different culture has a core which is common to all humanity—the differences are the contribution of each culture to the common experience and knowledge of mankind. This aspect of the differences in races and nations has not always been sufficiently stressed in the teaching of geography.

This brings us to the next point that knowledge in *itself* is not enough. Knowledge, in itself, will not necessarily give understanding. Still less will it necessarily give sympathy. There must be present an *emotional* attitude of mind favourable to this understanding and sympathy. The way in which a thing is learned, the way in which it is taught, are of prime importance to its emotional reactions. For instance, we would not trust too freely to the opinion of every Anglo-Indian on the thorny problem of Indian nationalism. The British soldier learning at first hand in France about the French people did not always learn to love them through this closer knowledge. Indeed, the reverse was frequently the case. Different British visitors to the United States will often vary diametrically in their conclusions about the Americans and their estimate of American psychology. It is not the thing seen, altogether, but the attitude of mind of the onlooker that largely decides the conclusion in a matter of this kind. The "grand tour" did not always prove an effective antidote to an insular point of view. Very often, indeed, it intensified it.

It is thus clear that mere factual knowledge will not give

world sympathy. Geography can so easily become the talking of a jargon about coloured shapes on a map or the repe-
tition of words in a book. As Fairgrieve says: "We must look
through the map at the country and people beyond. The map
is like a pair of binoculars—the more you look *at* it, the less
you see; the more you look *through* it, the more you see".[1]
  Where does this conclusion bring us? How can we teach
geography with the right emotional content so as to produce
the right reaction of human sympathy? How can we supplant
the active idea of competition with a more active one of co-
operation? The solution lies in the method of *treatment* in
the teaching of geography—a treatment not necessarily producing a *liking* so much as an *understanding* of other people.
It is necessary to make this distinction very clear. Too often
is it suggested that world conciliation depends on the development of a brotherly love for our "foreign" neighbours.
Rather is it this matter of *understanding* and of an unprejudiced
appreciation of the cold facts of the circumstances. World
co-operation, far from being a merely pious aim, is in reality
good hard-headed business.
  Dr George Green in his remarkable researches into racial
prejudices amongst school children suggests (and he does not
claim it as an entirely new suggestion) that the key to the
situation is the emphasis upon the idea of there being, for
instance, all over the world "people who do things for us".
Not that India "produces" so many tons of tea every year,
but rather that there are in India people who work in the
plantations to produce tea for *us*. We, of course, do something
in exchange for *them*, for example, make cotton goods for
their clothes. Money acts merely as the convenient medium
of exchange to facilitate this barter of goods and services. This
attitude in the economic side of geography, consistently followed at school, must result in a very different emotional
background towards the people of the world in the children
from that which is produced by the study, formally, of imposing statistical abstracts of imports and exports. Here
is perceived the fundamental likeness between peoples of

[1] At the conference of Educational Associations, January 1931.

different lands—that of service in a world community. The essential oneness of mankind is given its right place. Even if we cannot learn to *love* the worker in the plantation, we can at least learn that he is more a co-operator than a competitor; that he is a practical friend rather than a potential enemy. This is obviously so in spite of his colour, his smell, his hair, his ideas or any other of the lesser differences between him and us. We thus reach a realisation of him socially and avoid an anti-social prejudice against him.

At all costs, the fact of world interdependence and the actuality of modern economic co-operation, which is essential to modern civilisation, must be the basis of geography teaching. That reality of interdependence is there for all eyes to see—yet how few in the world do see it. It needs teachers sympathetic to this interpretation of world conditions. To the dry facts of the blue books must be added the emotional condition of the mind to see them in this human light. Geography must be taught with a consciously social rather than a negative background. The personal influence of the teacher must be of this character, and this is why the teacher's training is of such importance. This is where this series of booklets can carry a new message—and this message is not only a matter of the mind, but also of the heart.

III

WORLD COMMUNITY GEOGRAPHY
IN THE PRIMARY SCHOOL

BY J. LLOYD JONES

WHAT STRIKES ONE FIRST IN THE HUMAN FAMILY is its apparent diversity. Composed as it is of a variety of races differing in features, in certain habits, and to a large extent in language; varying in the degree of progress or of civilisation; living under widely differing climatic conditions, yet all members of this family are similar in one aim of life—the struggle for existence. This struggle again is characterised by differences in intensity. For the African, living in a humid tropical forest, nature often provides in abundance. For the Eskimo on the edge of the Arctic Seas, conditions are severe and the struggle is arduous. Periods of plenty are rare, and when they occur, they may be the reward of extreme toil or dangerous hazards. The favoured Temperate Zones, where human energy attains its maximum, present the problem of existence in a more complicated form. Here are found the most progressive races, and they have begun to harness the immense forces of nature to be subservient to their wills, and have succeeded in raising productive capacity to an incredible height. But political wisdom has not progressed hand in hand with scientific knowledge, and in these "civilised" countries stark poverty is rampant. Millions live below the poverty line, though the necessities of life are abundant, and all this is mainly on account of misunderstandings, jealousies, and unfriendliness between the nations. The problem before us, as teachers, is to explore the reasons underlying these misunderstandings, to build in the early years the foundation of a better understanding and to foster good and sound human relationships through, especially, our geography and history lessons. So far, geography teaching does not seem to have produced a real understanding in our children of the people and problems of the world.

It is a natural beginning in geography to speak of the time when life was simple and wants were few, emphasising the point that the earth and the sun are the ultimate sources of all the means of existence. Stories and illustrations descriptive of primitive man with his flocks and herds—parallel stories, and where possible, films, descriptive of similar conditions existing to-day—could be used to demonstrate human relationships in their simplest forms, then we can show that as civilisation progressed, wants multiplied and desires grew. The habit of producing only sufficient for family or group gradually changed and producers aimed at a surplus, to be exchanged for other commodities or to be sold for money;

thus was wealth increased and the standard of living raised. Thus were trade and commerce brought to the world. At first, trade was local and communal but there was a gradual development until it assumed international and universal dimensions. We can make it clear from our lessons that the basis of good trade is mutual satisfaction, and its continuance depends upon confidence and friendly relations between the parties concerned. Unless there is sympathy and good understanding these friendly relationships cannot develop. But good relationships depend upon accurate knowledge coupled with a sympathetic and understanding mind. A natural approach to this phase of the problem may be found in the study of familiar commodities. The breakfast table is a means of introducing to children many peoples and many lands. There is hardly a corner of the world to which the children may not vicariously adventure nor variety of climate or people which may not be discussed, and in varying degrees understood. With maps, charts and pictures, the pot of marmalade will give Spain a reality. The pictures will suggest to the children, when they see orange groves and lightly clad people working in the sunshine, much about the climatic conditions. Similarly the cup of tea will lead them on another adventure, and bring new peoples and new lands within their ken. It is an easy step then to ask how we pay for these things we enjoy. It will emerge that ours is a great manufacturing country with millions of people living in large towns. We cannot easily grow oranges, tea or cocoa, but the people who grow these necessities need machinery. They have not developed many factories for making cotton goods, or steel knives or many of the other things which we can easily supply. Thus do we trade with them. In days of prosperity our ships and those of others are busy carrying goods to and fro to effect this exchange, for which peace and confidence are necessary. The exchange is profitable to both parties.

It is in this connection that films can be of immense value and, could there be an interchange of films between various countries, it would help in fostering the knowledge and good understanding which are so essential to the functioning of world trade. Were we to continue in the Senior Classes to introduce in all our geography lessons this human element, this realisation of the interdependence of all the countries in the world, such a treatment should go far to dissipate the prejudices against foreign peoples that to-day exist even in children and even more so in adults, if we are to judge by our newspapers. There are people who wish to turn the clock back and who believe that world trade and commerce can be abolished in favour of a fabulous national economic life—that we can build, as it were, walls around every country and live independently without any outside contacts. In our teaching, projects may be worked out to show how dangerous this idea is and that life at its modern standards and extent would be practically impossible without world commercial intercourse. For instance, if a map of the world were taken, our own country being used as an example, and the children asked to name a number of things we could not do without, and if coloured tapes pinned at each end were used to illustrate this, we should find that Britain would be linked to practically every other country in the world. This in varying degrees can be shown to be true of almost every country in the world, yet the tendency to-day is towards the artificial restriction of this friendly and profitable commercial intercourse. To help in rebuilding a harassed world, whatever clogs the wheels of industry must be removed. When cotton is burnt in America, wool in Australia, coffee in Brazil, and other commodities destroyed in many countries, while at the same time millions of people are clamouring for these goods, and many are wretched because of sheer want, it becomes obviously a world problem of the first magnitude. We cannot expect to *solve* it in the Primary School, but we can at least lay the foundation for a better understanding. Seven or eight years of intelligent teaching with the teachers world conscious, and not nationally minded, could have a great deal of effect upon the next generation. Indeed it is only the teachers who can save the next generation.

A few ideas that may be helpful in framing schemes of work in geography with this in mind are as follows:

1. Geography should be introduced as a story of human activity in a varied world. Trailing familiar commodities to their sources, travelling there in imagination and seeing how the people live, making things like the Eskimo's igloo and kayak or like the African's kraal, witnessing films showing the habits and activities of people in other lands—this kind of treatment, properly handled, can do much to develop world sympathies in our pupils.

2. The children should study the home land, its commodities and people, why it is an industrial country, why so thickly populated, why our food supply is so scanty and why it is essential that we are on friendly terms with other countries. Thus the importance of raw material will emerge and the study of essential commodities like cotton, rubber, wheat coal, and oil will follow naturally. Maps and diagrams can then be drawn to show these commercial links. Films of industry and travel films of all kinds, if carefully selected, will make admirable illustrative material in a geography course of this kind.

3. The regional study of other lands, of their people, climate, soil and position with their resulting commodities will then be a logical development of the scheme. Commercial links between other countries and the home country when studied and understood will form, as it were, bridges of understanding between our people and the peoples of the world.

4. Then with this knowledge of the essential character of co-operation in the world's economy, the showing of how the League of Nations leads the way in encouraging co-operative action becomes both necessary and logical. The International Postal Union, the International Labour Organisation, the Court of International Justice, etc., then take their place in the scheme whereby man seeks to organise his world. But these organisations are in peril. Only the schools can save them if, in the race between education and catastrophe, education happens to win. And education cannot possibly win unless in the schools of the people the study of the world, which is Geography, is carried out with this actuality always in the minds of the teachers.

IV

THE FILM AND GEOGRAPHY TEACHING

BY GEORGE H. GREEN

THE PEOPLE WHO BELIEVE THAT CHILDREN CAN be educated by looking at films form, probably, a naïve minority of those who are interested in education. The number of people believing that nothing but harm can come of the film—either direct moral harm, or the injury to mental growth which may result from making the minimum demand upon the intellect—is greater. The attitude of many teachers seems to be a resultant of these two factors, varying as one or the other predominates. They believe that the film could teach a great deal. They believe it might do a great deal of harm. Hence many of them are still reluctant to use it, and some are openly hostile to it.

The teacher does himself a great injustice in speaking at all of what the film can do. He does not speak of what the blackboard or the text-book can do, but of what he himself can do with these aids. The film, whatever it is or whatever it may become, is not and cannot be, in the field of education, anything more than a teacher's tool. It is little more than the hammer and the chisel in the hands of the craftsman. What has to be considered is the form and purpose of the tool, and the technique which is to be developed in order that it may function to the best advantage.

The teacher stands always in a unique relation between a pupil and certain material. If looking at the material, or cataloguing it, or memorising it were all that is necessary, the teacher could be dispensed with altogether. It is the teacher's business, however, not merely to bid the pupil to look at the material, but to direct the looking; so that the pupil comes to acquire a point of view, not originating in himself but borrowed from the teacher, towards the material. The man who assembles together material in a book, imposing upon the marshalled facts not merely an order but also a point of view, is a teacher; as is the man who arranges, with a purpose in mind, the objects in a museum. The teacher of geography is in like case with his colleagues. Like them, he has an interest in the world of phenomena. Like them, he assumes a peculiar point of view towards certain of these phenomena. Like them, he wishes his pupils to acquire his point of view.

No pupil can make progress unless he acquaints himself with the facts; which are of fundamental, but not of paramount, importance. The facts which interest the geographer have been gathered by the slow progress of many men through the world. All the attempts made, in the classroom, to acquaint the pupil with the facts on which his study of geography must be based, are merely substitutes for journeys about the world—substitutes for first-hand observation of natural phenomena. The most fortunate schoolboy can journey to and fro in the world, and up and down in it, to a very limited extent only, and make only a very few observations at first hand.

The geography teacher is at a great disadvantage as compared with some of his colleagues, who, at least, can present directly to their pupils the phenomena they are discussing. The teacher of geography has had to fall back upon drawings, photos, stereograms, pictures of various kinds, narratives, and maps. The map itself is an aggregate of symbols, calling for a great deal of experience before its meaning is clear and immediate. Pictures and narratives alike are seldom exactly what the teacher feels that he requires, but he must use them as "next-best things" because nothing better is available. However good all these things may be, and however excellent the means for exhibiting them—light rooms and good wall spaces, frames and cases, optical lanterns and epidiascopes—we are compelled to admit that they are very far removed from the first-hand experience which is so desirable.

The cinematograph film, obtained by direct photography of natural scenes, is, it must be admitted, a great deal nearer first-hand experience of the world than any of the substitutes with which the teacher of geography has hitherto been provided. It does not mean that these other aids must henceforth be scrapped, but rather that they themselves will take on an augmented usefulness. The still photograph of, say, a mountain village or pass will mean far more to one who has actually travelled through the place than to one who has not: and it will, for the same reason, mean far more to a pupil who has experienced the illusion of journeying through it by means of the cinematograph film than for one whose experience is limited to the examination of the still picture. It seems clear, then, that the right films, properly used, do not merely provide the best substitute yet suggested for first-hand experience of the world, but at the same time increase the value of all the substitutes we have hitherto employed in the class-room.

The great weakness of the bulk of films produced, from the teacher's point of view, may be very simply stated. In them, the material presented, which might otherwise be so valuable from the geographer's point of view, has already had another point of view imposed upon it—"romance", as the producer understands the word. In the interests of romance the material has been arranged, until from the geographer's point of view it has become worthless: and not merely worthless, but false. From the point of view of "romance" it may be necessary to present Africa as a place in which widely separated peoples live in adjoining territory, where diverse natural features and geographical forms occur in amazing juxtaposition, and where film stars may rush about, unarmed and unguarded, for many days without any derangement of artificial complexions or physical discomforts—but it is obviously impossible to impose a geographical point of view upon material already so distorted in the interest of a very different purpose.

This criticism does not apply only to films manufactured with a "romantic" end in view. Many of the films described as "instructional", while less ridiculous, have been made for reasons which are not geographical, and are, for this reason, of little or no use to the teacher of geography. For example, it is clear that a film dealing with typical areas of a country may be of great use; whilst another, prepared in order to tempt people to emigrate to the country in question, may present a picture of the area which is, from the geographer's point of view, false. The teacher of geography will do well to examine carefully films which have been prepared for propaganda purposes, since they deal with material selected and arranged with objects in view which, however praiseworthy, are not geographical.

The criteria to be borne in mind have already been implied in what has been said. The only film which is of value to the teacher of geography is that which gives to the pupil a close approximation to actual first-hand contact with the earth, the home of man; and so acquaints him with the facts which are to be related to each other, through the agency of the teacher, in ways which aggregate them into the corpus of knowledge we term geography. We may add to this the film in which the geographer, as producer, has selected and ordered the material presented so that the film itself is geography. Such films are few in number, so that, in practice, the teacher will have to content himself with much that falls short of this ideal; but, if he bears in mind the purpose for which the film is to be used, he will be able to avoid material which will hamper rather than help him.

The technique of the use of the film must be determined by the nature of the medium itself, and by the purpose for which it is to be used. Obviously, its place is in the class-room itself; and its audience should be limited to the class. (The use of the film as a means of school entertainment is not under discussion here.) This means, in practice, that the film of most use is one whose exhibition will take up a part only of an ordinary lesson period, leaving time for discussion afterwards; in order that the material may not only be observed, but rightly interpreted.

A very real difficulty in the way of general adoption of the cinematograph as part of the regular school equipment is the economic one. Nevertheless, it is not difficult to acquire a good projector at a low price, since the general adoption of talking apparatus has thrown a great many serviceable second-hand "silent" machines on the market. Smaller machines, using "reduced" film, are on sale at low prices, and any good dealer is able to offer to-day machines at prices which are well within the reach of authorities and private individuals. Practicable cameras, with which the enthusiastic teacher of geography can make his own films, are also available. Attempts are being made, too, to develop library services of films and to place at the service of teachers the advice of experts in geography and the use of the film. The minor difficulties of darkening rooms, erecting screens, etc., can be overcome by ingenuity or, more easily, by the co-operation of the teacher of craftsmanship. Schools without an electric supply can generally obtain adequate illumination for an ordinary projector by using car batteries: or, where the apparatus is of small size, by a hand-driven generator.[1]

There is little doubt but that, as a real demand on the part of geography teachers for films of utility grows, the commercial producers will make intelligent endeavours to supply such films. Nor can we doubt but that, within a very few years, the cinematograph will be regarded as an essential piece of class-room apparatus; to be used, not indeed in every lesson, but as a matter of course, in all those lessons where its utilisation will be of benefit. So it will come to serve as another tool in the teacher's equipment, in no sense taking his place or making his teaching skill superfluous; but as something making further demands upon him, requiring him, for one thing, to attain mastery of the new instrument, for the further development of his craft and the bettering of his work.

[1] [An old motor-car engine with dynamo and batteries can in these days be obtained, literally for a song, from the breaking-up yards or garages. With the addition of an extra water tank for cooling, installations to generate electricity for use with small film projectors, and optical lanterns, and with listening apparatus can be set up in country schools. It will be well to seek the advice of electricians and motor engineers when doing this. Editor.]

V

GENERAL CONSIDERATIONS ON THE FRAMING OF SCHEMES OF WORK ON GEOGRAPHY IN THE ELEMENTARY SCHOOLS

BY FREDERIC EVANS

IN CHAPTER I, DR GEORGE H. GREEN HAS DISCUSSED the evidence which shows that amongst school children, and therefore also amongst average adults, there exist in their minds dangerous misconceptions, prejudices and inaccuracies concerning the peoples of other lands. Of this fact there can be no shadow of doubt, for this prejudice against "the foreigner" is widely exhibited in the popular press read without criticism or even doubt by an equally prejudiced public. Many publicly exhibited films[1] show this prejudice too. For example, as Dr Green has shown elsewhere, the child view of a Chinaman is often bound up with opium dens and sinister cruelties. Of the millions of peaceful home-loving Chinese peasants there seems to be little permanently fixed in the minds of the children. These demonstrable facts are both an indictment of and a challenge to our schools.

In Chapter II Miss Celia Evans has shown that a mere factual treatment will not reach the truth—that wisdom, as apart from mere knowledge, has an emotional aspect and that facts taught with the wrong emotional background can give rise to prejudiced and therefore incorrect conclusions. The teacher has to be in sympathy with the world and the problems of its peoples. This does not imply that frank opinions should not be expressed if these are based with knowledge upon the widest possible foundations.

In Chapter IV Dr Green discusses films and pictures as

---

[1] It is fair, however, to refer to films like "Kamaradschaft", "The Man I Killed", "War is Hell" and others, which make for greater understanding and sympathy between peoples.

invaluable illustrative material for the teaching of accurate geography. Films showing the life of different peoples in action cannot but have a profound educative effect upon children seeing them, but here again their discussion by the teacher must be sympathetic and not flippant. Not, for instance, that the African rickshaw runner is absurd in his head decoration of oxen horns but that it is only a sign of his work as a transporteer, derived from the extensive use of oxen as beasts of burden in Africa. If the teacher can refer to similar absurdities in our own lives as seen in the eyes of the "foreigner" so much the better, especially if such impressions can be quoted or translated from original sources. The habit of self-criticism and of a tolerant irony in the young generations of that Britain which "first at Heaven's command arose from out the azure main", will do much to open their eyes to our own shortcomings and to realise how, often, what seems to be obviously right to us, frequently appears high-handed and cynical to other observers. To the Chinaman the European peoples are known as the "White Peril".

The film can do much to dispel what is the bane both of history and geography teaching—that of reducing countries to elementary types by way of extreme simplification. The types then tend to become caricatures and to omit references to diversities and variations so that people often think of other countries and their inhabitants in fixed, inflexible terms. They may think in connection with history, for example, of the French as grasping, or of the Germans as arrogant, forgetting their many human qualities, and the contributions made to culture by these peoples and by all nations. Or in geography, the children must not visualise the Dutchman, for example, merely as a picturesque sabotted figure standing before a background of windmills. He is *a* Dutchman not *the* Dutchman. This personification of peoples into convenient caricatures is largely due to an excessive zeal for rushing early into generalisations. Generalisations in geography as in everything else must come at the very last, after years spent in the appreciation of accurate selected information about the phenomena in, and the peoples inhabiting this variegated world of ours. Indeed, there are many generalisations which can be omitted altogether and left to mature during life. At any rate they must not be forced. The "reason why" geography has tended to produce immature reasoning and over simplification. This side of geography can, as far as the more intricate generalisations are concerned, be left to the senior school stage, that is, when the children are over eleven years of age and even then in the latter year or so, when the threads of the children's accumulated knowledge can safely be gathered into organised wholes.

What then on framing syllabuses must the teacher have in mind at the different stages? There are, of course, no syllabuses which can be termed final. They will vary in content with different considerations and with different teachers. After all, in education we can only select from an infinitely wide body of knowledge, yet in the selection we must have regard for essentials and use these in a manner fitting to the ages and interests of the children. We can never "cover the ground" we can only plot modest itineraries through the vast fields of knowledge.

In the Infant School, the children's interests and understanding will centre round simple things in their own geographical environment. Their way to school, elementary ideas of direction, of size, of day and night, of the change of the seasons, and the characters of the months, of heat and cold, of sun and cloud, of ice, snow and rain, of wet days and dry and of all these things in simple combination. Then come the personal figures in their social environment which play a part in their economic life—the milkman, the grocer, the postman, the butcher, the baker and so on. The co-operative organisations or society will later become apparent to them. Then of other lands, perhaps in the latest stages, simple folk-tales can be told, acted and read. Folk-tales selected to express incidentally the geographical circumstances should be used, but there should be no attempt to ask for complex reasons for anything. It would be legitimate, for instance, to ask why the Russian *Isvoschik* in the story wore a quilted coat but not why is it so cold in Russia. In all this work there must be no suggestion of patronage in the expressions or even in the tone of voice of the teacher. Young children have no class consciousness whatsoever but they will quickly absorb suggestion even if only unconscious or subtle, of superiority over others. The fairy-tale and the folk-tale breathe the spirit of the early days of civilisation when there was a greater consciousness of the essential oneness of mankind.

The Primary School work would follow naturally out of the Infant School preparation. In Chapter III Mr Lloyd Jones has discussed a method of approaching the teaching of geography in the Primary School from the angle of world commodities leading to ideas of the interdependence of the countries of the world. This is a very practical method of approach. It may be of interest also to give briefly a syllabus of geographical reading based upon the ascertained interests of children in the Primary School. No reference is made to essential work to be done by the teacher in simple weather lore, in the simple study of the neighbourhood, its land forms and its maps and in the study of the homeland in a simple way, as these are not pertinent to the particular purpose of this booklet. But teachers will understand that their lessons would be complementary to the children's reading on the lines of the scheme given below and these lessons could with advantage be based on the ideas described in Chapter III. For instance in Stage III below, the internal exchange of goods and services in the homeland can be stressed, and in Stage IV their exchange for commodities from other countries of the world discussed.

GEOGRAPHY READING SCHEME

STANDARD I (7–8 years)

Folk-tales of all lands giving, incidentally, much geographical colour and background. (Of rather harder type than those used in the Infant School.)

These stories could be both of the type which can be read by the children themselves and those which only can be read by the teacher to the class.

STANDARD II (8–9 years)

Stories of the animals of the world—for the animals reflect unerringly the geographical conditions of their environment. Climate, geology and vegetation would in a simple manner emerge indirectly from such stories if well chosen. Besides, to children at this age, animals are, demonstrably, a dominant interest.

STANDARD III (9–10 years)

Stories of the people in the British Isles who *do* things—that is, of the co-operators in our economic and social life. The stories should describe typical individuals—spoken of personally by name in a narrative giving the sense of romance, of adventure and of the joy of doing in their lives. E.g. "David Morgan—the Collier", or "John Brown—Engine Driver". The stories should be of a kind in which the geographical factors would appear quite incidentally and naturally.

STANDARD IV (10–11 years)

Stories of people all over the world who *do* things. These must be real yarns in which the geographical settings emerge naturally as part of the story and the treatment generally would be like that described in Stage III.

These "geography readers"[1] should be readable for the sake of their general interest and should first and foremost tell a tale. The lesson of geography should not be stressed but should be in the background. Books of this character—as many of them at each stage as possible—would both give the kind of geographical information which it is the Primary School's business to provide, and also be sound in human sympathy and understanding—sympathy with animals—sympathy with all sorts and conditions of men. It may, in passing, be said that the teaching of the *structure* of geography is the teachers own job in the Primary and Senior Schools and the reading should be supplementary rather than used in attempting to give formal instruction in the subject.

Coming to the Senior Schools, the children will then be

---

[1] A series based on this scheme is in course of preparation.

ready for a more scientific and formal study of the geography of the world. They will be more ready for principles if these, where they are complicated, have not been attempted previously and at too early a stage. The mass of information sympathetically acquired in the Primary School through suitable reading, suitable pictures, suitable talks, etc., will begin to sort itself out under the expert guidance of the teacher. The beginnings of organised human geographical knowledge become thereupon possible.

There are of course numerous syllabuses which for this stage can be planned. As a matter of interest a typical one can be given in outline:

SPECIMEN SYLLABUS FOR SENIOR SCHOOLS

FORM I (11–12 years)

The simpler Continents, i.e. Africa and South America. These are studied at this stage because in these continents the simpler regional types are fairly clearly marked and life in them is least altered in character by industrialisation. This of course has to be understood only in a relative sense as civilisation is altering and has altered life in these Continents in many ways. Their links with Britain should be traced.

FORM II (12–13 years)

The Monsoon lands and the Antipodes, i.e. Regional types having some peculiar characteristics. Their links with Britain.

FORM III (13–14 years)

Europe and North America, i.e. the highly industrialised and altered Continents.

(If the leaving age is 14+ then at this stage also would come a more scientific study of the homeland and its relation to the rest of the world in general and to these Continents in particular.)

FORM IV (14–15 years)

The British Isles and the World, i.e. a scientific study of our own islands and their links with the rest of the world in commerce, colonisation, emigration, science, finance, etc.

It will be noted that the British Empire is not studied in the above scheme as if it were a separate geographical unit, but its component parts would be dealt with at each stage as they are met when studying the large divisions of the world as shown in the syllabus.

Similarly the place of the League of Nations in World Geography would come in its proper perspective. There would be, as each region is dealt with, consideration of the geographical problems with their political repercussions—e.g. Manchuria, the oil regions of Persia, the coaling stations, the ship canals and so on. The territorial problems of the world would have to be discussed, frankly, but in no spirit of jingoism. The habit of looking facts in the face and of judging them judicially needs to be fostered, but above all, these problems should be approached with all humility and with tolerance and sympathy.

The mandated territories in which the League is interested under its covenant and the fate of this new experiment in political control should in their place receive special attention in the geography lessons we visualise. The problems of minorities and frontiers, the restrictions of trade and the counteracting effects of political divisions between areas fundamentally one in economic life should be discussed with all the detachment of which the teacher is capable. Then there are in this "international" aspect of geography the problems of commerce, of the free ports, of the internationalised rivers and so on. And why not also a consideration of the economic effects of diseases all over the world and of the efforts made by scientists of all nations in combating them, and especially the enormous work on these lines made possible by the activities of the League of Nations? The International Postal Union, the international air routes and their control, the International Labour Organisation—these in the nature of things all must have close relation with any modern treatment of geography.

This implies in the Senior School or classes a deeper knowledge than perhaps the average class teacher possesses. A specialist system may provide people qualified to undertake this work, but much can otherwise be done by systematic reading. Reference is made in the next chapter to a few books which will help materially the teacher in this work. Especial attention is drawn to the source book on "international geography" which will give valuable information on the points above discussed.

But whatever scheme is followed it must deal with people and not merely with places, statistics and things. It must deal with them sympathetically, for, as Miss Celia Evans says, it "is not only a matter of the mind, but also of the heart".

VI
MISCELLANEOUS INFORMATION
BOOKS

A Handbook for Geography Teachers. (Edited by D. A. Forsaith.) Methuen. 4s. (Goldsmith's College Handbooks for Teachers.) Is a recent and authoritative publication which contains useful discussion, suggested syllabuses and lists of selected books for the teaching of Geography and for the Geography teacher.

It also contains chapters by G. J. Cons, M.A., on "Teaching of International Geography" and on "Geography and the League of Nations". This book should be in every school library and in the hands of every teacher of Geography.

A Source Book for League of Nations Geography. Is in course of preparation by the Geography Panel of the League of Nations Union, Education Committee. It is being edited by G. J. Cons, M.A., and will shortly be published. It will contain extracts from League and other official documents concerning Mandates, Health, Minorities, Transit, Communications, etc., and will show how widespread are the activities of the League throughout the world.

The League of Nations and the Schools. Board of Education, Educational Pamphlet No. 90 (1932). 6d.

The League of Nations in Theory and Practice. (C. K. Webster and S. Herbert.) Geo. Allen and Unwin, Ltd. 10s.

Ten Years of World Co-operation. Geo. Allen and Unwin, Ltd.

Ten Years Life of the League of Nations. (Compiled by John Eppstein.) The May Fair Press. 7s. 6d.

The Dawn of World Order. (Nowell Smith and Maxwell Garnett.) Oxford University Press. 3s. 6d.

Teachers and World Peace. League of Nations Union. 15 Grosvenor Crescent, S.W. 1. 6d.

Suggestions for the Consideration of Teachers. Board of Education, 1927. 2s. Note particularly Chapter IV on "Geography" and Appendix B on "The League of Nations".

League of Nations Maps. Various modern maps published by the League of Nations Union. These show mandated territories and frontiers as changed by the Treaty of Versailles.

The Aims and Organisation of the League of Nations. Geo. Allen and Unwin, Ltd., 1928. Publication intended for Elementary and Secondary school teachers.

The United World. (Sherman & Spaul.) Dent. 1s. 9d.

Geography in Education and Citizenship. (W. H. Barker.) University of London Press. 6s.

Report of Geography Panel. League of Nations Union, Education Committee. 15 Grosvenor Crescent, S.W. 1. (Pamphlet.)

"Memorandum on the Teaching of Geography in Secondary Schools." By a Joint Committee of Assistant Masters in Public and Secondary Schools. Geo. Philip and Son, Ltd. 3s. 6d.

SOCIETIES

THE LEAGUE OF NATIONS UNION, 15 Grosvenor Crescent, S.W. 1—for information, pamphlets, advice and assistance on all matters connected with the League of Nations. For Wales, enquiries should be addressed to

The Welsh National Council, 10 Museum Place, Cardiff. Particulars of suitable summer schools both in this country and abroad are obtainable from the Offices of the Union.

THE GEOGRAPHICAL ASSOCIATION. c/o Department of Geography, Municipal School of Commerce, Manchester. Of assistance to all teachers of Geography. Annual subscription 5s. The publications issued by the Association, of book lists, model syllabuses, etc., are most valuable.

THE NEW EDUCATION FELLOWSHIP (English Section). 29 Tavistock Square, London, W.C. 1.

"*The World To-day*, calls for concentration of educational effort throughout the world, since no merely national movement is in itself sufficient to meet the present crisis. Only through education in its widest sense can we hope to produce a new society capable of making proper use of the machinery for international co-operation which is now being set up in every field. A new attitude is required in all educational work, of which the following are the essential points:

(1) Education should equip us to understand the complexities of modern social and economic life, safeguarding freedom of discussion by the development of the scientific spirit.

(2) It should make adequate provision for meeting diverse intellectual and emotional needs of different individuals, and should afford constant opportunity for active self-expression.

(3) It should help us to adjust ourselves voluntarily to social requirements, replacing the discipline of fear and punishment by the development of intelligent initiative and responsibility.

(4) It should promote collaboration between all members of the community. This is only possible where teachers and taught alike understand the value of diversity of character and independent judgment.

(5) It should help us to appreciate our own national heritage and to welcome the unique contribution that every other national group can make to the culture of the world. The creation of world citizens is as important for the safety of modern civilisation as the creation of national citizens."

The Fellowship publishes *The New Era*, price 6*d.* monthly.

THE SCHOOL JOURNEY ASSOCIATION—which is interested in journeys to the Continent. Hon. Sec., H. W. Barter, 35 Parkview Road, Addiscombe, Croydon.

THE JUNIOR RED CROSS SOCIETY. Has international associations and does much international work. Address: 14 Grosvenor Crescent, London, S.W. 1.

INTERNATIONAL EDUCATIONAL SOCIETY. Hon. Sec., K. Garrett, 98 Clerkenwell Road, London, E.C.

WORLD EXPLORERS, LTD. This association specialises in the encouragement of travel for youths on the continent of Europe. Address: "The Friendship", Charing Cross Pier, London, W.C.

AUXILIARY AIDS

BROADCASTS TO SCHOOLS. The Central Council for School Broadcasting arrange regular broadcast lessons to schools on geographical and other subjects of international interests. (Address: c/o B.B.C. Broadcasting House, London, W. 1.) Booklets with full particulars are regularly published.

THE COMMISSION ON EDUCATIONAL AND CULTURAL FILMS. Address: 15 Taviton Street, London, W.C. 1. This body exists to advise on the use of films in Schools and detailed information may be obtained on application to the Secretary. Under the auspices of the British Institute of Adult Education a quarterly magazine— *Sight and Sound*—is published at 1*s.* and is a valuable source of information on this branch of Education.

THE CENTRAL EDUCATIONAL DEPARTMENT. 98 Clerkenwell Road, London, E.C. 1. The Combined Educational Departments of the Columbia, and the H.M.V.
Gramophone Companies Records of interest to students
of languages, music, geography etc. are available.

OTHER SCHOOL ACTIVITIES

These are discussed in detail in the little booklet *Teachers
and World Peace* in which work geographical in character is
included. The following are a few auxiliary methods of aiding
the "international" aspect of geography teaching.

Making Costumes of various Nations in the Crafts lessons
after designing them in the Art lessons and searching for
knowledge of them in the geography projects.

Foreign Correspondence and Exchanges with children in
other lands. The League of Nations Union can assist in
arranging suitable contacts. Exchanges of teachers and even
pupils have been arranged by some schools.

Travel Clubs and Youth Movements, also journeys organised under the auspices of the School Journey Association.

The Performing of Plays with a setting in another country.
This work will need some geographical research, especially
in connection with the design of scenery, costume and
properties.

The Music of the World. Used in Concerts in the School.
Characteristics may have a geographical aspect and the music
and geography classes can here co-operate in a valuable
project.

Junior Branches of the League of Nations Union can be
formed in Schools. For particulars application should be
made to 15 Grosvenor Crescent, S.W. 1, or, in Wales, to
10 Museum Place, Cardiff.

MAKING CONTACTS

WIRELESS MESSAGE OF THE CHILDREN OF WALES
TO THE CHILDREN OF THE WORLD

The children of the schools of Wales have since 1922 broadcast annually to the children in all the countries of the World a message of goodwill. This is done on May the 18th in each year, or Goodwill Day, this being the anniversary of the First Hague Conference of 18th May 1899.

The Message now results in thousands of replies from children in every land. For 1933 the message read as follows:

BOYS AND GIRLS OF ALL NATIONS, WE, THE CHILDREN OF WALES, ONCE AGAIN WARMLY GREET YOU ON GOODWILL DAY.

IN THIS SPRINGTIME OF 1933 THERE ARE, ALL OVER THE EARTH, MILLIONS OF CHILDREN WHO ARE UNHAPPY BECAUSE THEIR FATHERS AND BROTHERS HAVE NO WORK TO DO. WE DO NOT KNOW WHY THERE SHOULD BE SO MUCH SORROW IN A WORLD WHICH IS SO BEAUTIFUL AND SO MUCH WANT IN A WORLD WHICH IS SO RICH.

WE BELIEVE THAT THIS WOULD NOT HAPPEN IF ALL THE NATIONS TO WHICH WE BELONG WOULD LIVE AND WORK TOGETHER AS MEMBERS OF ONE FAMILY TRUSTING EACH OTHER AND ENJOYING TOGETHER THE RICHES OF THE EARTH. WE BELIEVE, TOO, THAT BY OUR THOUGHTS WE CAN HELP TO BRING THIS NEW SPIRIT INTO THE WORLD.

LET US THEN ON THIS GOODWILL DAY, MILLIONS AND MILLIONS OF US, UNITE IN ONE GREAT THOUGHT OF PEACE, PEACE BETWEEN THE PEOPLES AND PEACE BETWEEN THE NATIONS. WITH THE FAITH THAT CAN REMOVE MOUNTAINS OUR THOUGHTS WILL CHANGE THE WORLD.

A booklet describing this message and its story is obtainable, free, from Mr Gwilym Davies, M.A., 10 Museum Place, Cardiff. This message and the replies can, obviously, be used to great effect in both the geography lesson proper, and in the work of school societies like Junior Branches of the League of Nations Union, the Junior Red Cross, and other Youth Groups.

VII

A NOTE ON THE USE OF TIME CHARTS IN THE TEACHING OF GEOGRAPHY

BY FREDERIC EVANS

WITHIN THE GENERAL TERM "GEOGRAPHY" there is historical geography in which the influences of geographical environment upon the events of history are traced and there is the history of the study of geography and of world discovery. Both these aspects of the subject may be included in a geography syllabus in the senior stages.

Thus in the "Geography Room", if such a room can be organised in the school, there should be a "Line of Time" consisting of uniform sections of paper ruled to mark the centuries from a few hundred years B.C. to the present day. These sections should be pinned at about eye level around the blank walls of the room and as the lessons on the history of geography and of the discoveries are taken, labels and suitable pictures would be affixed in the appropriate places on the Line of Time. In this way a correct relation of these events to each other in time would be established and the chart would, if kept in clear outline, be an excellent source for revision.

The chart is best built up as the lessons unfold themselves, rather than be put up on the wall complete in every detail. It is important that the names of events and persons be marked clearly on the chart with indicator points showing their correct positions on the time line. There should be portraits and other illustrative material affixed appropriately to the chart to give a pictorial outline of the subjects dealt with and also clear simple sketch maps are obviously suitable for the same purpose. At the same time the Line of Time should not be made too elaborate—it should deal with essentials and not be overcrowded with detail. Newspaper and other cuttings often form useful additions to such charts.

Such a Line of Time will help to show more than anything

else our debt to scientists and explorers from all over the world. In no study is the result of the combined efforts of people from different nations to be seen better than in the story of the study of geography and of the discovery of the world. In World Community Geography the use of the Line of Time is, therefore, of supreme importance.

VIII

THE WORLD CHANGE

BY H. G. WELLS[1]

CONSIDER HOW PEOPLE LIVED IN ENGLAND OR France or any other country in the sixteenth or seventeenth century. They ate, they drank, they worked and played, they lived in houses that didn't look so verydifferent from the houses we live in now, their furniture was similar to ours, they had clothes, sometimes more picturesque and elaborate, but otherwise very like the clothes we wear. But their food and drink—with the possible exception of a bottle of wine or so—were produced within a few miles; their tools and playthings were all made nearby; their houses were built of material found in the neighbourhood; their furniture and clothes were equally home products. In a prosperous English home then you might find nothing that came from outside the country except perhaps a little silk, some spice, a bit of gold or a precious stone. The country was a complete system in itself. If in those days England had been cut off completely from all other countries, if all the other countries had ceased to exist, had been entirely de-populated and cut off from England, people in England could have gone on eating, drinking, working and playing, sheltering themselves and clothing themselves in the way they were accustomed to, with only the slightest changes. And the size of the boundaries and the scope of governments of those days were adapted to that condition of things. England and France

[1] Reprinted with the kind permission of the author and of the publishers of "The Way to World Peace" (Ernest Benn, Ltd.).

and Spain and Portugal were really independent of each other and could get along at a pinch without each other. Each was a little world in itself—into which patriotism fitted beautifully.

But to-day all that is changed—except that the size and boundaries of England, France, Spain and Portugal remain almost the same.

To-day a large part of our food and drink comes from countries beyond our boundaries and some of it comes from the ends of the earth. We have altered our way of living and become accustomed to a greater variety of foods and our populations have increased beyond the capacity of our national food supply. Need I recite a list of the familiar things that would vanish from our homes if suddenly all that we owe to importation were to disappear; tea, coffee, chocolate, oranges, lemons, bananas, most of our bread, most of our meat, and so on. And equally with our clothing. We should find ourselves half stripped. The car in the garage would become immobilised for want of petrol and our telephone useless for want of copper derived from imported ores. And no effort to adjust things and make our forty odd million people suffice for themselves would save us. The crops in our fields would wither if the nourishment they had received through imported fertilisers were withdrawn. Seven-eighths of our industries would stop short, through lack of this or that necessary ingredient, metal, fatty substance, oil or what not. And that would throw most of our population out of employment. Everything would be dislocated.

Thus, instead of belonging, as our great-great-grandparents did, to a comparatively simple local economic community, almost completely self-sustaining within its national boundaries, we have become members of a vaguely defined world-wide economic community. The other parts of the planet have become necessary to us as they were never necessary to our great-great-grandparents, and we and what we do and produce have become necessary to the other parts of the world. This process of the extension and intermingling of needs and interests is still going on very rapidly. We are rapidly becoming one world-wide community of interdependent human beings.

TEACHERS AND EDUCATION FOR WORLD PEACE & CO-OPERATION

"GEOGRAPHY"

"After history, geography is the school subject to which most of this new body of knowledge naturally belongs. Pupils should be led to realise the conditions of life, as well of individuals as of communities, among the nations of the world, and especially among those peoples with whom we in Great Britain have most in common; and proper emphasis should be laid upon the economic interdependence of the Great Society, now almost world-wide, of which we form a part. And, of course, every school should possess a wall map showing the old and new political boundaries and demilitarised zones of Western Europe, and another to show the mandated territories and the altered frontiers in Africa and the Middle East."

The above is an Extract from the Declaration of the Teaching Profession in, "The Schools of Britain and the Peace of the World"—(1927). The Declaration is signed by representatives of the National Union of Teachers, the Educational Institute of Scotland, the Headmasters' Conference, The Incorporated Association of Headmasters, the Incorporated Association of Headmistresses, the Incorporated Association of Assistant Masters, the Incorporated Association of Assistant Mistresses, the Training College Association, and the Council of Principals of Training Colleges.

For EU product safety concerns, contact us at Calle de José Abascal, 56–1°, 28003 Madrid, Spain or eugpsr@cambridge.org.

www.ingramcontent.com/pod-product-compliance
Ingram Content Group UK Ltd.
Pitfield, Milton Keynes, MK11 3LW, UK
UKHW012335130625
459647UK00009B/309